the sunflo

the sunflower project

unLYSHed

to The I Am Who *is* Love
the man who *enkindled* love
and the woman
who found love

table of contents

sowing

withering

budding

unLYSHing

i thought that He would make me like a bird
that He would give me wings to soar above my troubles
i thought He would make me like a mountain
stubbornly unmoved despite the rain
instead
He made me a sunflower
rooted in Him
resiliency built in my stem
one petal for every part of my truth – a truth that continues to be
discovered
and then at my core
the heart that forgives
that overcomes
that continuously tracks the Son
He gave me purpose for my being
this is where it begins

sowing

u n L Y S H e d

the sunrise
is my favorite good morning kiss

good morning
the cocks are crowing
the dew curls in comfort on the blades of grass
the morning star undresses before the night sky
you lift your head
you take your first conscious breath
grant freedom to your smile and
snuggle your sheets
before the soles of your feet meet the wool of your carpeted floor
you groom
you tame your mess of kinks and curls
you wash away the bed
you dress
in your girlish frills
the ones embroidered with your heart
you spritz your skin with clouds of dreams
you sit
you create
you paint the beautiful world in which you wish to exist then
blow against the canvas until it dries as your reality
you don't move
until
it has dried as your reality
then you eat
consume your daily bowl of purity
and savor the tang of naivety intertwined with your imagination
you tie the ribbon around your hair
you say one sided prayers
of gratefulness for the day that you believed in
for
the morning that
you chose
to see
you are beautiful
but you are
blind

u n L Y S H e d

there is a light within her
she has yet to understand

my Father wrapped me in skin
planted me in the plush grounding
of my mother's flesh
folded His blessings
into her womb
the first safe place in which i was fortunate enough to exist
where i first experienced
what it was like

to be held

and she did hold me

even when from within her body
where i absorbed her aliments
and sprouted and stretched to her discomfort
even when i became too big for her insides and she was forced to give
of her strength
to bring me to light
even *though* i took
even *when* i took
she gave
with a smile that teemed with pride
it was then
that she held me

she still holds me

the beginning of my love story

u n L Y S H e d

i remember
when life was like chocolate chip cookies
its sweet and salivating aroma tiptoed around my nostrils
baiting me for an experience that would surely
spark magic on my tongue
i was anxious for the timer to tick
so that i could have a taste
and then all i wanted was
bite after bite

the sunflower project

they look at us and say
you all have the same face
i reply
it's bigger than that

we all share the same heart

      family

my first best friends
are the reason for
my favorite memories
my worst scoldings
and the kind of laughs that caused our sides to tremble
in sign of ultimate bliss
they are responsible for the becoming of the
protector
defender
and nurturer in me
for them i would visit the pits of hell
for them i would give up my heart
for without them
it would be of no use to me

brothers

when we pray
we all touch
the connection of flesh to flesh
under the purpose of
meeting with the King
activates the portal that brings
Him into our midst
we go one by one
lay at His feet
and watch as grandma's house
fades away
we unravel into the most
exposed versions of ourselves
and soon are resting at
the throne of grace
in God's presence
we unmask our truth
surrounded by one another
we unmask our truth
confessing
professing
praising
we cry a cleansing river on
which we sail back to this
world
holding one another
when the tears have stopped
the experience commenced
and we open our eyes
we are again
in one of the safest places on earth –
grandma's house

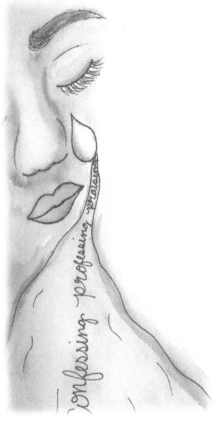

when they wonder why we are so close

as a little girl
i would be excited to close my eyes
just to wake the next morning
to see my mother's face
to smell my daddy's coffee
to hold my brothers' hands
to give my grandmother kisses
to dance on my grandfather's feet
and to be passed from one uncle's arms to the next
i could not wait to wake up
to feel and be
loved

the sunflower project

money was short
but love ran the length of the oceans

childhood

my father and mother slept peacefully
in the room across the hall
they left on the light for my brothers and me
just
in case we had bad dreams
daddy made us breakfast
mama read us stories
they both
always said goodnight
i empathize with you
on the absence of one parent or the other
my heart is capable
of feeling your pains
although   they   are
pains
i have not felt
before

love
like you are stretching your petals
exposing your center
and feeling the sunlight tingling in your skin
for the very first time
love
like you've been underwater and
you've just come up for your first gasp of air
love like you're bursting
like it's painful to withhold even a portion of what you have to give
love hungrily
love fiercely
love gently
love intensely
love like if you don't
your core will wither and fade
love the way that love was given to you

life for life

she is
fire
a combustion of the breath of life and
the potential in her body
craving the day of its ignition
she's ablaze
and she draws a crowd
her presence
is terrifying
and welcoming
threatening and warm
crackling and cozy
the older she gets
the brighter she burns

i was just a little girl
when i discovered
the flower pressed between layers of
my flesh
hidden in the secret garden behind the
gates my legs created
i was taught that some will come
who
will want to see how this flower sways
if its center swells and quivers
in response to their fingers against its
stem
they will want to taste
the nectar that it can produce
and that my curiosity
may wish to let them in
mother and grandmother told me
let them stand at the gates and wonder
let your flower be their mystery
they did state
that the God Who lives in my heart
connected its roots to the roots of this flower
He
will select the one
meant to pick it
not to be rid of it
but to protect it
cherish it
and to enjoy its beauty
i was warned
that it's better He do the choosing
than i

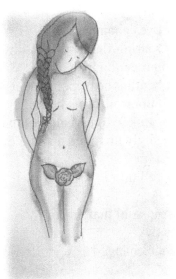

this day
her eyes changed
her roaring flame retracted with a softness
upon meeting his gaze
her beating heart pounded as he approached
and it purred at his hello
she blinked to reveal eyes that sparkled
and shyly unveiled a smile that glowed
this day
she fell into love
he
was in soul mate form
this day
things changed

7.31.10

i let you break through my skin
and though my veins were stubborn
you tied me off with your efforts until they finally produced an entry
way for you
you took advantage
gave me a shot of your love
it was
tenacious
ambitious
it spread like wildfire
it was
purposeful
strategic
it changed my blood type
immediately
i knew i had always
needed you
truth
i was raised not to abuse substances
but
i've never felt a high like this and
all i can think of is
how much more of you i want
and i want to feel how you make me feel
for the rest of my life
it has to be you
your hands
your lips
your smile
your eyes
your secrets

your fears
your pains
your plans
your future
with me

give me more
your loving sends me into a frenzy
you whisk me away with your strength into our happily ever after
you've impressed yourself into my mind
stitched yourself to my brain now
i constantly think of you
you stand guard in my dreams
you come to me each time that i need you
and i now realize
that i could never not need you
when we're apart
my heartbeat rises but
the lullaby of the professions of your love for me play
in your voice over and over until my anxiety is replaced with a certain
peace
if i'm still enough

i feel your fingertips against my skin just
lightly enough to make my body respond in quivers
when i close my eyes
i see your image
with your love for me hidden in your breastplate
carrying the sword of my spirit that
heals you
in your hand
i see your eyes locked onto the depiction our forever
and i believe in you
as everything about you says you know
what you are fighting for
it was me
that you were fighting for
the promises you've made me are branded into my palms
i hold them there with your heart
and in return you
make me high
you supply my ride to inexplicable euphoria
and i trust you
to meet me at my peak with your loyalties
to catch me in arms cushioned with your covenant
to squeeze me with passion until we both explode
i have no intentions on returning to sobriety
i'd rather
stay up here with you
i'd rather stay up here with you
so tell me you love me
say it again
pull me so close that our skin blends into an endless stream of caramel
wonder
hold my face like you're cuddling with fragility
bite my lip with the gentle intensity that both unsettles and excites me
and

join me
let me do the same for you
i need you here
i need a constant supply of your affections consistently laced with trust
i need you to never run out for me
i need you to never run out on me
if you cut me off
i might stop breathing
my body is used to having you
living inside me
i have grown to function only if
there are traces of you in every sacred part of me
i'll be fine
as long
as i
have you

the sunflower project

when you touch me
how you touch me
i can't control the flood

u n L Y S H e d

there is no possible way to measure
the number of times i
thanked God for you

the sunflower project

you were never in a rush
when you met me
you came close enough to inhale my scent
from there you learned the things that make me wild
when you leaned in for our first kiss
you did not try to consume me,
but rather brushed your lips against mine with a gentle graze
enough to make me wonder how your tongue would feel as guest in my
mouth
then you cradled me
to lay me beside you
as this was the perfect position to rock away my fears before
you made love to my ambition penetrating it with your validation
this was
pleasure
we took our time
and parented a new creature

love that was true

it was a wonder how beautifully you fit into my puzzle

missing peace

the sunflower project

i considered myself favored -
wrapped in frills and ribbons
having *you* amid this dying world
after braving it alone
i had been gifted
to a partner
and a lover
in you

the fluttering of butterfly wings
shooed hunger into a quiet corner
kisses
created a thirst for more kisses
the reality
of his existence
created a storm that fell from my eyelids
his arms
provided shelter -
protected me from loneliness
i trusted them to always remain
he was
necessity

overdosing

the sunflower project

they warned me
careful, baby girl
you are still so young
you never write anymore
you never go out anymore
it was then
i taught myself to hide
from the people who knew me most
it was then
i decided
he loved me
best

hallucinating

u n L Y S H e d

i do not know when
but at some point
i had to have asked God to scoot over
i had to have lain down to make my body man's red carpet
that led to God's seat in my heart

his footsteps almost crushed me

      idolizing

the sunflower project

i found out you were lying
you only impersonated the lover i knew was
set aside for me
that reality was the ugliest beast i had ever beheld
that the happiness you created for me had been through simulation
that you were capable of mutilating my heart
by way of deception
yet i could not believe that
none of it
was real
when you removed the frames
when the broken glass was brushed away
you stood before me as a much different version
of a man
i was still in love with

this was when i should have left

u n L Y S H e d

he knew he had my heart secure
he then made a play for my mind

       this was when you should have left

the sunflower project

it did not matter what he did or said to me
i could not turn the love off

      even after he did

u n L Y S H e d

something about my determination to be kept
excited him
i'm sure he challenged himself
let's see how much she can take

the first time
i heard God speak to me
clearly
He was interjecting to address
an offense i placed on Him
"God, i want to be loved"
"is My love not enough"

u n L Y S H e d

his earliest insult was focused on my skin
you're really not my kind of beautiful
he taunted
you've had too much sunlight
it would be years
before i would rediscover
the beauty in the beams i carried
but in that moment
my mind wondered
how to get them out

  bleach or blade

the thought of him leaving me
made me like a fish out of water
it sucked the oxygen from earth's atmosphere
and left me gasping painfully for my breath
my knees shattered against the ground
i lay squirming as each part of me shut down
one
by one

he liked to watch

unLYSHed

your words
oh, how they burned me
and when i cried out in agony
you trapped my screams behind the hand
you slapped across my mouth
after you told me they were unattractive
you whispered
look – i'm the only one who loves you anyway

the sunflower project

this is what you prefer
to think for me
to speak for me
to recreate me
how boring we became
you labeled my inquisition as stupidity
marked my creativity as feeble
declared it a sin to feel or believe
differently than you
as if you were the only one of us
who was worthy of existence
as if the best thing for me was to become
swallowed up by you

       essentially
          i dove down your throat

the best way to describe what we turned into
is to describe the puppet and the puppeteer
he reached inside of me
grabbed on to my heart
he spoke into it
he gave me permission to speak *only that which left his lips*
words
in my voice
masked with his influence
he pulled my heart's reins
to move me to please him
i bended to his will
like my spine was as weak
as a dandelion stem
i transformed into
exactly who he allowed me
to be

the sunflower project

before long
i refused to look
in the mirror
i knew
looking back at me
would be

u n L Y S H e d

i cut off my fingers
plucked my eyes from their sockets
the search for new ways to love him
demanded i show
i had no love for myself
i committed to the sleuthing and
fell apart

the sunflower project

i was praying
but i was doing it wrong
"God fix it"
His response
"that's not My will"
i never heard Him

selective hearing

the thing about planting
is that it is the genesis
a seed does not know its revelation
when it is only a seed
when a sunflower sprouts her first layer of petals
she does not know that more will form
when the sun burns the sunflower's back
she does not know it can warm her face
until she is turning
the idea
is to be content as a seed
but not attached to the seed state
rather it is to be excited when transformation comes
even if it hurts
even if it's ugly
even if time ticks with stubbornness
even if it brings you close to death
you must come to be full in the state you are in and
simultaneously be fully
becoming

it's not over yet

withering

how dare you leave me

i enthroned you
i bathed you in my ever flowing well of adoration
and pinned my praises together to form your crown
i massaged you in oil
meant to penetrate your pain til it dissipated into a memory
i wiped your insecurities onto my skin
caressed your temples til your worries alleviated your body and
stained my hands
i made your bed of velvet and rose petals
cradled your head as you lie down to rest
prayed for your dreams to drip in honey that i would package and
prepare for you to garnish the breakfast that would meet you each
morning you gifted me with the opening of your eyes
i made you
majesty
how dare you leave me
you used to touch me
you were
so gentle
so
intentional
you passed through the canal to my heart as if you built it yourself
and you took note of the detail
you learned me
studied my interior until you memorized my design
so closely that you found spaces that could be filled with you
and you did
fill me with you
you would fall into me at every glance, losing yourself in my presence
before landing in the sea of my passion for you
you told me
you enjoyed the fall

when you tattooed me with your affections
and whispered how committed you were to
keeping and protecting me forever
i wore you in my skin with pride
it started to hurt
i embraced the pain
trusting in the beauty of us as a perfected work
an idea you etched into me and
i trusted you
you became a part of me and
i carried you
you became too much for me but
i needed you
you knew i needed you
that connection revealed your savagery
you tasted blood in the water
your eyes changed
you re-emerged as a creature
seeking to devour
us
and you did
rip us apart
you shredded our always
after sinking your teeth into
me
you pierced more than my flesh
you cut through my psyche
closed your jaw around my frame
til i was relieved of my goodness which leaked onto you
now you release me
with shards of what made my soul beautiful between your incisors
you depart from me to make a home with another when your actions
have me incapable of even
lifting my head

you'd leave me like this
as the mess you made
as if i could be loved by another
this way
who knew
i would kiss the lips of the reaper
made weak by
loving you
why was it so difficult
to continue to love me
why were you amused
by owning me
enslaving me
attacking me
then
leaving me for dead
you knew
i'd give up everything for you
i gave up my everything for you

the sunflower project

i hate that my mama raised me to be the kind of lady
that shouldn't show a man when he has broken her heart
the times where your disappointments invoked my anger
i wanted to become the woman
who would drive 300 miles to close my fingers around your throat while
i dug my fingernails into your soul
bruised it with my grip -
squeezed it to my pleasure
all before goading you to ever try to live without me
i should have come
it would have felt better to respond in violence
crying
begging
waiting
pining were all
so much worse

      i failed her either way

the phrase
time heals all wounds
is a manmade concept
that gives false hope
as if the hands on the clock would leave their post
as if minutes and seconds would be the needle and thread that
stitched me back together after you'd ripped your way out of me
i hadn't seen you in months
but when i looked at you
loving someone else
before i knew it
i was knee deep in a puddle of my own blood

she was wearing my
smile

God did not have to command woman to love
it is written into her genetic make up
to give of herself
fully
God *did* warn woman to protect her heart
because He knew
that man
wouldn't
He knew
that she would be eager to give it away
that scripture was one i had forgotten
instead of giving my broken heart to Him
i kept forcing it onto you

    i'm the one i needed protection from

u n L Y S H e d

i don't know which i miss most
your heart
or your hands

    without both

the sunflower project

~~dear lover~~
dear abuser,

why

u n L Y S H e d

it took more and more from me *to continue to reach for you*
i wanted to be filled
and to be felt
instead i kept drawing back
less and less of myself

    butchered

the sunflower project

i knew you reserved the right to reject me
it surprised me that you exercised it

u n L Y S H e d

how odd is it
that i continuously watched you
giving what i wanted
to the one you chose
when you called
i still answered
when you wished to come over
the door was left unlocked
and when you told the world
about her
i took a front row seat
how odd is it
that i had become so devoted to you
and so detached from myself
that i would take you
 in any form

self-inflicted pain

the sunflower project

i never tasted a tongue
that pleased me and pained me like yours

kisses and offenses

u n L Y S H e d

i knew i was in your heart
that's why i was shocked to find her

in your eyes

the sunflower project

the first time i accepted discomfort
in order to appease you
you explored my private parts
your finger was unwelcome
but you pushed through anyway
i remember
not understanding that pain
that night under cleansing water
i touched and was allowed entry
to a place i had not been before
when i realized what had happened -
that you had begun to make me a woman
instead of saying i was not okay
instead of confessing
that i was fine with being a little girl
instead of entertaining the question that rang in my ears:
what about Daddy
i let my shower rinse away my tears
i labeled your action as a thing that grown-ups do
acknowledging it as necessary
to keep
you

      i was playing dress up

u n L Y S H e d

i deprived myself water
denied my access to the sunlight
how ruthless was i
to invoke the withering
just to stay in the dry season with you

the sunflower project

you shoot your words at me like daggers
they pierce my ego
carve away at my confidence
puncture my spunk
the more they work
the duller i become

and they still won't make me

her

       the one you wanted

u n L Y S H e d

why didn't you just go

      word to us both

the sunflower project

you said there was no other that moved you like me

    liar

u n L Y S H e d

he's hurting you, they say
my small, weedy voice
escapes the sobbing
to declare
i love him

he doesn't love you

if i stay, *he'll love me again*

       22 pounds lighter

the sunflower project

did you feel like a god
egressing your now shrunken flesh from my body
were you satisfied that you had conquered what was seemingly
unconquerable
that must have been how you felt
when you stood over me
lying naked in a strange bed
as a strange guest
with strangers
waiting outside for you to finish
when you stuffed your manhood in your pants
preparing to go out for the night
preparing to leave me there alone
you *must* have felt like a god
to know my mouth was incapable of asking you to stop
but faintly able to beg you to stay

first time

u n L Y S H e d

what makes me most anxious
is that i don't know why i can't release you
it's harder and harder to remember how you loved me
what was so great
between the
insults
the lies
that i cannot let you go

the sunflower project

love
is meant to be shown
not in word
but in deed
if his tongue produces
i love you
but his words sting like bees
if his hands are wild
and stifling like weeds
if he is not present for the sake of your garden's upkeep
then his mouth is full of dandelion fuzz
thick with fluff and
nothingness

u n L Y S H e d

it wasn't fair
how my body betrayed me
i got up from his bed
tears still on my face
but days after i left him
i woke with an unusual tingling
the sunflowers between my legs were
begging to be stroked
i had always wanted him
but this want was different from before
i hated
that i would love finding him
there

crossover

maybe i should have asked as a little girl
why does God say no to this
as a woman
i can tell myself
your body will want more
and man will willingly give it to you
but man may choose not to stay
and man after man
will hurt your soul
they will leave behind pieces of themselves that are lifeless
they will be heavy inside you
fatigue from carrying the weight will show in your eyes
you were not meant to be reduced to a pavilion
made a shelter for wanderers
your blueprint makes a home
the inhabitants besides God
are the husband He chooses to love you always
and the children that will blossom within
if you wait - you will not be without pain
if you do not
your pain will be different
your body will demand attention
that you will want it to have
but every man was not meant to taste you
and as each comes and leaves
they take with them some of you too

you offered me a tightly wrapped wad of earth
to place between my lips
to take into my body
to burn its way down my throat
at first
i shook my head
no
then you spoke again
if i were going to share this with anyone, i would share it with you
i almost snatched it from your hand
i did not care to smoke
but to score the opportunity
to be the woman
you would share a smoke with
as if
this was a sign of love
as if
this was a sign of affection
as if sharing in this with you
made me more of the woman
with whom
you wanted to be
the substance was not my
choice of poison –
you were

i'd do it all for

YOU.

    higher

the sunflower project

even after almost losing my life to the strength of your waves
if you would calm for me
i would dive into you
all over again
i'm not sure if i'm merely obsessed with the waters
or if i truly love to swim

    drowning

u n L Y S H e d

i waited for you
the same way an abandoned child waits for an absent parent
with hope
without a doubt
for years

you never came back for me

the sunflower project

when men gaze at me
they don't see their equal
they see their prey
how then does that make me look

u n L Y S H e d

dear LYSH,

what's wrong with you

the sunflower project

i still had you on my hands when i reached for another

   filthy

u n L Y S H e d

i should've waited for the *i love you*
before i let them in
instead without passwords
i admitted visitors who would dance with me to their climax only to
depart before my favorite song
and so
i was left to dance
alone

      speak*: easy*

the sunflower project

i made myself believe
you were understudy to one i would soon meet
i held auditions
looking for him
i was posing as the director
i was acting like the prop

i should have been concerned with my own character

unLYSHed

the fruit of my lost loves
makes my jaw clench
leaves a film across my lips
and is sour on my tongue
do i blame them for giving me bitter
or myself
for taking a bite

questions

no
i did not meet your ear with screams
did not claw my way from your grasp
did not kick
did not speak
my
tongue had
been cut away long before you came along
my mouth
still full of blood
i *couldn't* give you my consent
i know
i didn't give you my consent

u n L Y S H e d

when he finished
i cried in silence

he didn't even know my name

my Daddy had taught me better
i was not living like the reflection of Him i was called to be
i decided
it was best that i not trouble Him with my transgressions
it was best that i keep my shame to myself

this was my folly

un L Y S H e d

waiting to be wanted
has been the kind of painful
that spoons everything good thought i once believed about myself
out of every part of my mind

i disposed of them all

    soiled

the sunflower project

still no prayer

u n L Y S H e d

there are times
when i want you so badly
my desires erupt in my belly and crawl upward towards my mouth
they find their exit barred –
my lips are not allowed to release pleas for you
the enflamed yearnings
are untamed
they *screech*
they *claw*
but remain trapped inside

they never rest

third degree burns

the sunflower project

truth
i've never broken a lover's heart
just pieces of my own
i used the shards to shape myself into
his ultimate desire

u n L Y S H e d

sometimes
i would remember my fire
how embarrassed former me would be
to look at me now
i would not face myself
it was best that i hide
i'm sure she would demand i show her a woman
i had no idea how to be anymore

the sunflower project

trying to replace you
was a subtle form of suicide
i cannot even measure
the amount of life i allowed them to take

walking dead

this is the result of living broken
you are like a tornado
of slivers of your own soul
the debris it creates makes a trail behind you
you leave what is truly *you* behind
and pick up the dust and ruins you pass over
your light becomes
dimmer
although you desperately
want to shine
the potential is there
for your garden to grow again
it needs you to feed it
it needs you to tend to it
it will not flourish
without your attention

the sunflower project

i made a habit out of lying next to him
i was surprised at how good he would feel to me
and at the places
he could carry me
i knew he would never be with me for long
but as long as he remained i would
let myself
indulge

delusion

u n L Y S H e d

i started with good intentions
wanting things to go my way
but when he took the wheel
i let his detour show me things
i had not seen

joy ride

the sunflower project

he started a new battle i would struggle to fight

me vs lust

i was the kind of addict
that claimed to want cleanliness
and hung out on my old block
i wanted to be known
i wanted to be loved
but i had been reprogrammed
to please
no matter what it cost me
when they smiled at me
i smiled back
when they kissed me
i did not run
when they touched me
i became uncomfortable
silent alarms went off in my body
but i was incapacitated as a result of my drunkenness
it was more difficult to speak
with my lips locked onto his
i must have looked like i wanted to
by the time he snatched my clothing i was deep into my stupor
i remember
wanting to say *wait*
and not being able to move
so i lay there
while he borrowed my body
wondering
how *hello*
somehow drove me
to my old block

the sunflower project

at least
the animals that are feasted on in the street
are already dead
i felt every rip and tear of my flesh
and heard my soul screech in pain as it became
my lovers' lunch
i was not dead
but just as lifeless

      roadkill

u n L Y S H e d

why fight so hard
why not accept that i am
a pit stop for those finding themselves
why not make theirs a memorable stay
why not believe
that i am only
what they have made me to feel

    unworthy

the sunflower project

for the time they would spend holding me
parting my lips to plant their kisses
extending warmth from their bodies to heat my own
for starting their mornings wanting me closer to them
sliding their hands across my sheets pulling me into their arms
for the chance to pretend they were mine
for the chance to pretend that it was real
i became submissive
my performance stunned even me

unLYSHed

this is not power
allowing man to soothe his itch,
absorbing the moisture from *my* petals
then validating sharing my tenderness
allowing *him* to supply a knock off brand of nourishment
who decided
that this exchange
was
healthy

the sunflower project

i started having my coffee at night
i needed to meet the sandman at my window
to implore him
to keep his distance
i dealt with *my* thoughts
i acknowledged *their* actions
but the haunting was just an unnatural punishing
my lovers past would visit me
to press me into my mattress
to mock me and to pass me
from one pair of hands to the next
the tormenting in my sleep was even worse than reality
i could not escape the withering
not even in my subconscious
rest was withheld and
sleep had become the gateway to torment

i would rather stay awake

u n L Y S H e d

each time my love story begins to bud
the earth beneath it gives way
do i stop trying to bloom
or become the thorn it would rather make of me

the sunflower project

all this time
in all these years
no one i wanted has wanted
to be with me
to watch the seasons change

u n L Y S H e d

i felt as if my petals
were being relieved of their brilliance
made colorless
and fragile
then ripped off of me
the withering was painful
it was making me numb
i was too weak to make it stop
so
Daddy did it for me
and when the love-me-nots ceased from falling from my interior
i found time to catch my breath
breathing was like rehab
like i had been going without oxygen
like drugs were being purged from my system
like my body was so used to hoarding the things killing me
it could not support life
and so it seized
the loneliness was so strong
it knocked me to my face
the itch to be touched
so intense
i scratched scars into my body next to the
ones my lovers left
this cleansing continued
it pulled from within me
more thoughts of being unwanted
and more thoughts of being unworthy
and more thoughts of being dysfunctional
until I asked God to change my mind
i asked Him to clothe it rightly
it was then i became grateful for the isolation

hope yet

the sunflower project

had He not stopped them from coming
i'm sure i would be
a headline

brain dead

u n L Y S H e d

i was just getting to my feet
just smiling again
just settling again
finding something great to live for
returning to God prodigally
looking for myself
reaching for my pen
i almost touched it
but i was distracted
the enemy visited me
there was always war
but the next shots were launched
on my house

    personal

the sunflower project

this is what the enemy does
he tempts us with sin that suits our tastebuds
he strikes the space in our heart that we would protect with our lives
it was no different for me
he asked for my mother
for my aunts
for my uncle
he asked for my heart
i prayed with valiance
i prayed with vigor
for total alleviation from his wiles
i prayed the prayers of david
i prayed the prayers of job
i prayed with the kind of surety
that Elijah had for the rain
with great hope
and great confidence
i prayed for deliverance

i never got the peace i wanted

u n L Y S H e d

what do you do
when it looks like
the enemy has won

the sunflower project

i sucked for air
that did not satisfy my need to breathe
processing
what had been told me
"he's not coming home"

     suffocating

unLYSHed

this is not the world in which i wished to exist

i thought i had been angry before
i wanted to demand answers from God
to shout at Him
why
how could You
what now
i don't understand
but being angry took energy
i had none
i woke up
i stood while the day moved around me
i put on the mask that showed my smile
and i stayed silent
this time
it was not because my tongue had been cut away
but because i had no idea what to say

        lost

u n L Y S H e d

this is what we do
when our faith is weak
we
don't
we don't move
we don't pray
we don't try
oh, but we cry
and inside we boil
with our questions
with our doubts
without our hope
this is where the enemy wants us
in question about the existence of the God we claim is real
i was there
with the people of faith barely planted
i was there as a result of digression
i was there with the people who
feel pain
experience loss
and then
stop
as if there is nothing left in which to believe

we were wrong

when they asked if i was okay
i wanted to respond
that i felt that the reason for having my being had been crumbled up
then pressed with heated iron
passing as "*good as new*"
as if the warmth from the metal
would remove its creases
and its dents
it wanted to pose as unblemished
but in reality
it was damaged and
i didn't know how to fix it
yet
i chose to reply
"God is good"

      but i couldn't find Him

budding

the stage was properly set for my faith to bud
in the soil of Who my mother professed God to be
fertilized by my grandfather's sermons
irrigated in my witness of the lives of the church folk
and yet
they were not enough to dissolve my outer shell
to reach my core
or to activate the potential for true and boundless relationship with God
at rest within me
He became mine in darkness
when the harvest was scarce
when the season was dry
when the ground was cold and choking out life
but since then when i am in darkness
i feel closest to Him
it is there
that i thank Him for the darkness
for without the darkness
i would only have my mother's professions and my grandfather's
sermons
the right soil
the right food
and the kind of roots that were not
deep enough into the earth to hold
me throughout time
within the darkness
i found the love that brings forth the
Light
because of the darkness
He is mine

u n L Y S H e d

it started with Him
   it will end with Him

one day
i woke
the lights were turned on and revealed the second spirit alive within
me
i was
offended
that someone else was occupying the space of my body and of my
mind
with me completely oblivious
i pondered on the times i felt i was in darkness
on if those could be times that i rested while she reigned,
i thought specifically
of the hard**ship**
of how the crew mocked my mother's
deafening cries
of how the deck was stained with my grandmother's excruciating
pains
and of how the fog of my and my siblings' fear
lingered and
bullied us into a corner
before the storm set our sail of faith on *fire*
amidst the sabotage
i had been pushed overboard and i realized
it was her
she was there
and while i was sinking
she was
building
busy using my *preferences* for deliverance and edited versions of
God's word to prepare our avoidance of the flames
she refused to consider humility
or suffering

or endurance as forewarned in His book of truth,
but fashioned her tools from
miracles
favor
and rainbows
as if one part of His word held more power than the other
as if each element did not work together as one
she constructed for God her desired exit strategy without consulting
God for His will
not knowing that His will
included the flames
and as it was done, without *my* permission –
when He didn't fit behind the barricade of my own logic and
understanding
when His will encompassed going through the valley of the shadow of
death
instead of fearing no evil
i created her
and then i
became cold
took off my faith to
inspect it
study it
neither wear it, nor dispose of it but
try to understand it
understand what it had become
all i *felt* was anger
all i *felt* was forsaken
and all i felt was *wrong*
i could not figure out how to exist with reality and righteousness
so i became
frozen
my hope
concentrated within my core and hardened

its rigidity extended itself to the outer parts of my body
snowflakes formed on my skin
the sparkle was sucked from my eyes
and like ice we had been picked
to withstand the flames
like a weakling
i shrunk away
and left *her*
to stand for *me*
as a heap of ice chips and cowardice
i looked at my bloodstained hands
i found that even as a believer
i had limited understanding of what it meant
to *wait* on this God
depend on this God
or rather
to trust in this God
i felt like peter
when the cock had crowed thrice
the audacity of me
to run away from the God that i knew
from the Savior i loved
abandon the gift in my family
at the first sign of hardship
from rock bottom, i fell on my face
parted my lips to sing His praises like i had been taught as a little girl
but with the intensity of a woman who now knew pain
i cried out to Him to restart my clock
rescue me and carry me from my self-centered ravine back to reality
where He was shaping me
and asked that while He shaped me if He'd be kind enough to restore
me
then to appoint me as a warrior strapped with the responsibility to
always

love Him
choose Him
serve Him
despite the flames
as my mouth released those petitions
i opened my eyes
took my spot amongst the ranks with my bloodline
the blaze had intensified and
lapped at everyone i loved
it taunted us with its thunderous question
WHERE
IS
YOUR GOD
we crouched together
we cried together
we touched and we prayed
together
and after we had suffered –
we had to suffer, but
after we had suffered
we felt God blowing away the raging devourer
He was finally calming the flames
though i had split, He lent His grace to me
that i could again, *stand*
Daddy had allowed the fire, but He kept His word –
He didn't allow us to burn

the sunflower project

this was the beginning of finding more petals
and appreciating the ones already in existence

      rediscovering self

un L Y S H e d

dear God,

of the 756,864,000 seconds i have been alive i spent 4 questioning your existence
in those 4 seconds i licked insanity like it dripped down the sides of an ice cream cone
it passed my tastebuds, trickled poison into my soul and
i withered
died
slowly
quietly
gladly
i would rather expedite dying
than to live life with no purpose
than to exist without the existence of perfect and unconditional love
than to be left here to face this earth with no one to go home to after death
it took four seconds for me to crumble
 despite a lifetime of faith
and yet
when You rebuilt me
wait
You still
rebuilt me

the sunflower project

there was a time
i packed what was left of myself
and prepared to run away
God snatched my plane ticket
the force knocked me over
but i didn't meet the ground
i kept falling
til i landed in the same arms of the same people that had carried me
i didn't realize how weak i was
or
how badly
i needed them to carry me

home

unLYSHed

sisters
are meant to suffer with you
to fight with you
to heal with you
to pray with you
biologically
we could not be
but we needed each other for times like these
so God appointed us
to a status of our own

"*Shoo*"

i finally picked up my pen
i held it for a short while
the power i felt from
returning to my norm
startled me
but the tingling in my fingertips
was a sign
there was work to be done
i was anxious
to admit it all
to show my
contrition
to apologize
to externalize the
internal storm
i was anxious
to tell my Daddy

dear God

u n L Y S H e d

my grandmother taught me
when i have no words
to give God my groaning
my moaning
and my tears
it's a language to Him
which the Savior interprets into articulation
of my pains
and once my wailing falls on my Daddy's ears
He
moves

rescue

it makes me
a different kind of weak in the
knees
to find that when i drug my faith
to the middle of the sea
tied to it stones of
ungratefulness and rejection
and tossed it to its doom
You drained the ocean of its
waters
at rock bottom
 i found it again
in Your special way You
reminded me
that it would always be me and
You
that there was nothing You
would not do
to have me with You

how i love to be loved

unLYSHed

there was a need to tend to the gardens
both in my spirit and in my flesh

the sunflower project

i looked at myself
and was terrified to see *their* faces
in place of my own
it was then
i realized my addiction had gotten the best of me
i was finally sober
but still
i was not
myself
the trade involved
my identity
for their affections
the high was long gone
and so was i

        intervention

un L Y S H e d

it's time to face the monsters

dear daddy
i owe you an apology
for dancing with men who could never hold me
the way you've held my mother
who did not exemplify the same patience you did
when teaching me to tie my shoes
i owe you an apology
i insulted the way you've protected me
by welcoming crooks into my quarters
they stole from me
but i dishonored you

like father
like son
is one of the most repeated sayings heard in this lifetime
it indicates that a man's male offspring is likely to look and behave
like him, and i must say
i see the family resemblance
i see that you look like a man who
chose to welcome sexual stimulations he did not ask for and
was much too young to experience, who
forced bad touches into sensational touches, who
seasoned his discomfort to taste like his pleasure
who then cooked it up in best sellers and *fed it to you*
you
who were born and bred a bad seed
you ingested that which was stale - appealing on the outside but soiled
on the inside
his number one hit dish digested, rested in your insides and now look
at you
rotten to the core
i checked out lifetime's surviving r. kelly, and
realized in his lifetime he raised up generations of juniors
i heard a few i knew called him "daddy"
you ask, "how dare he do such things to little girls?"
but last i checked
innocence wasn't only measured in age, but also calculated in the sum
parts of the mind
adult body, in an adult world, but one + one didn't make me *too* much
closer to adulthood
at 19 i still pulled out my coloring books
still
shaded my world green
green for gullibly

trusting that you might have liked me
for looking at you and thinking, *"oh he's cute,"*
for drawing your name in the pages of my notebook, i
didn't know
that having a *crush* gave you the right to *crush*
my love fantasy
that a wink in my direction permitted you to take my body into your
custody and you were
careful to mirandize me when i protested with my heart
i didn't know you would dine on the physical, knowing i would choke
on my *"please stop"*
that you would wash down your victory with the saltwater from my
pillow
or that the morning after i would vomit all the things i really wanted to
say, like:
i like you
but
don't you want to get to know me
why don't you take me on a date
this is unfamiliar territory
this is going too fast
i don't want you to enter my body
i don't want our souls to make the unbreakable bond
don't want to spend the rest of my life *trying to forget you*
don't want to feel forced into promiscuity, attempting to keep the
power *you want to take*
don't want to convince myself
that i'm not so special
but that an experience with me is one for
any who's interested
don't want you to *haunt me in my dreams* -
to creep in the sacred depths and crevices of my mind
leave footprints on my eyelids
or remembrances that assemble in drops of liquid fire

crawling from my tear ducts burning streaks into my cheeks
don't want to open my eyes and gasp for my breath
choke on the ashes and find my lips singed with your names
i don't want to have to survive

I DON'T WANT TO HAVE SEX

when the latina woman said
"next thing i knew his tongue was in my mouth and i didn't know
what to do,"
i
felt
that -

and you knew, didn't you?
and you told me
when after my deflowering you made light of my sacred transition by
imploring me to "*settle down*" when i mentioned relationship
again,
when you exited my temple and said with conviction that *i wasn't the
girl you would marry,*
and again
when you rested atop my pillows and told me you had no ulterior
motive for your time with me,
you showed me you knew and that
he taught you
he taught you the game, and how to pick the ones that
didn't know how to play
i know i should've run away
should've fled
like jonah
but i became like aaliyah and chose to rock the boat
you refused to make me one in a million but *i* needed a resolution
i fumbled on the play of my comeback strategy

i took a page from *your* daddy's book,
tried to learn like you
i wanted to make it okay
i found that other colors better suited my worldview but refused to
look
i kept picking up green
telling myself this will all be worth it, the day he becomes my
boyfriend
i can make him love me
if i keep letting him come over
so i opened to door to my heart
moved the clutter blocking the space for you out of my sight
tucked away my God's written point of view on love
closed up my photo albums of adequate depictions of monogamy
swept my dignity under the rug with my desires
then stood at its opening with arms wide open and i
waited for you
waited for you to claim your not so grand prize, and
while i waited
the seasons changed
the wind chill from the breeze *froze my bones*
my knees got tired and *gave*
my cranium met the concrete and my good senses pooled beneath my
body, carrying away my
self-worth which was hand in hand with my innocence, and any hope i
had for you –
i lay there for years
stagnant – *still*
just recently i pulled out my coloring books
now, i rarely use green
it's been some time now
but sometimes now
i touch my crown and the pain shoots through my body
the kickback forces me to tremble

i find myself becoming nauseous, i
get a little lightheaded and right before i fall i'm
reminded of you
and how you look like your daddy
you even go so far as to tell me
i'm all grown up now, and that i
"used to be so innocent"
makes me wish that you were bulimic
makes me *wish* you'd give it all back
that you'd choose *better*
that you'd think *harder*
that you truly knew the ultimate Father
but you didn't
and He and i were out of touch so - *i don't blame you*
you were just
being a *good boy*
filling your daddy's shoes
like father
like son

the sunflower project

we were both broken
but our pieces together did not create
anything more
than a mess

u n L Y S H e d

i told her
everything
and i could see the love clawing from her eyelids where i assumed
shame would be
i guess
i forgot to whom i was speaking

     mama

the cleansing

dip me in bleach
scrub me til my soul bleeds
rinse me in healing waters
that i may be cleansed of you
i want the fumes of the strongest cleansing agents to burn the residue of your
cologne from my nostrils
need them to pressure wash my hippocampus so that there are no remnants of
your stay
need them to decompose the parts of my cerebellum that are stamped with
your blood
i need to be cleansed of you
take me to the jordan stream
submerge me beneath its current
raise me up that i might sacrifice the parts of you that clung to me to rock
bottom *to drown*
i want to be free of you
i want to take my breath on the other side
and inhale for the first time in a long time because your love was suffocating
and i had chosen
to live with
no air
i don't want you to haunt me anymore
i'm exorcising your ghost
it's lingering here but you're living –
you're only *dead to me*
you stopped seeing me as worthy
you made me believe i wasn't worthy
and you caught me
a repeat offender charged with
wanting you despite
but that didn't give you the right
to punish me
cruelly and unusually
i can't believe you made me watch
that you ensured that i would see you choose *her* over me,
then *her* over me, then her and her until it was her over me

and tell me
who is she
over
me
she could never have more time
our happiness was intact long before her invasion –
even after you welcomed her into our home
where she tracked our halls with her prints
for years
you continued to *lay with me*
she could never have more pain
i was accustomed to your sadistic experimentations
before you caught word of her existence
you'd find ways to kill me from the inside
practice one and revive me for the next while *i lay without resistance* for the
sake of your pleasure
and i'm still dying
each time you knock down my doors
checking to see if my pulse still drums to the sound of your name
resurrecting the possibility of *us* in my brain
offering a life you refused to support
as if she could ever love you more
as if she could offer you the eye of life's hurricane while leaving herself to
drown
as if she could ever be the kindling beneath your potential that burns in
unremitting *belief in you*
as if any lover could ever be comparable to me
when i set up daily conferences with God on how to help *Him* exalt *you*
at the cost of my own liberation
this is me
and i've loved you with an attitude
she's in your bed
and i'm still wreaking havoc in your head
as
the one you claim you need
that reminds you of who you are and *who you want to be* and
those words

were *yours*
they ran from your lips
and found rest on my ears as
a truth you rarely tell
and though i love you
i hate you
not only because you chose something different for yourself
but
because you could've lifted your foot from my neck
you could've left me
let me find my way to my feet and maneuver in darkness til my world
without you made sense
but you lingered in the shadows
whispered my favorite lies when i became stronger than you thought i should
be on my own
and when my smile curled in ways you never caused it to
you touched me and you know
i love your hands on me
i was a surgeon's guinea pig for you
so you raised the table with your untruths
picked me apart took what you needed and your favorite pieces to date *come*
from my heart
it's no wonder i'm drawn to you
you've got fractions of my insides stapled to your chest, for which
you must think you're superhuman as with
no effort
no commitment
no intentions on making things right
it's been proven that you have rights to the best parts of me
but
i tire of you gutting me open just to leave me to bleed
and it hurts the most because
you could have saved me
substituted your scalpel for your needle and
stitched me up with commitment
could've *loved me back to health* and been granted more
could have made equal deposits

and gained access to greater withdrawals
but you refused to see my value
and would rather *rob me of my life*
you don't
get
to have
my life
or to say that i'm not worth *today*
that i'm not worth now
or to be patient
to watch you live your life and sit in waiting *while you run from me*
run from the wholeness that you feel with me and
run from the man you have the potential to be
the man that *i* project to you when you look at me
you're a **coward** –
and i don't want you settling for me
or thinking
that i'm an option and that this is multiple choice
i know you thought that with me you would always have home
but your *uncertainty and confusion*
with your *betrayal and disillusion*
doused the foundation in gasoline
at your last let down
a match was struck
the *absence* of your love caused the ceilings to cave
the *crying* in place of the laughter busted the windows
the floors are *too weak* to hold us both
one more touch and the walls will fold like dominoes
the painting of our once blissful existence has faded beyond recognition and
in addition
i told God
that i desperately

don't want to love you anymore

so tonight
i'm taking my butterflies

and i'm *setting them on fire*
they'll have their last flutter over the space in my heart that used to be *ours*
as the embers fall and the flames squeeze our once safe haven
i'll grieve you
grieve *us*
but i couldn't sustain what we had alone and
i'll watch til we are burned to nothing
i'll watch til we are burned to nothing
atop the ashes the tombstone will read

*here lies the remnants of what was almost a dangerously intense,
recklessly stable, terribly fanatical, erupting and potent, world shaking,
heart throbbing, confident, sturdy, trusting, healing, exemplary, divinely
orchestrated, everlasting*

love

it'll be there for you to visit when you need passion in place of the
commonplace
you chose
over
us
and i won't be there
i won't even remember the spot
i'll have been cleansed of you

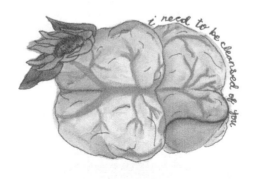

u n L Y S H e d

she holds you so tightly
because when she reaches for your heart
at the spot she's yet to touch
she cringes in pain
her fingers are scorched
by the flame in you that dances for me
she holds you so tightly
because she wants you to feel her
more than you love me
she need not try so hard

    my absence should make things easier

the sunflower project

you were my favorite weed in my garden
though you would pop up against my will
i would always let you stay long enough to choke up
everything i was growing to be

    no more

un L Y S H e d

you marvel at the parts of me you never knew
i point them out one by one
this flower sprouted when you left the first time
these came each time you came back to leave again
i did not understand their existence
but they look beautiful to me now
then i walk you to the cemetery behind my heart
i show you the pieces i once grieved over
all the former parts of me now dead because of
you

i do not care that you are proud

the sunflower project

it does not matter
if and how much i love you
i am no longer interested in acting on either

unLYSHed

he will love me the way that you should have

the sunflower project

you know that tomorrow isn't promised
yet continuously give her every today
it says a lot to me that if you were to take your last breath
you would want to do it
in her arms

    letting go

on the mornings i wake up energized, i spend a little extra time thanking
God
i know He ran me through your dreams
allowed me to stain your subconscious with my lipstick
wouldn't let you sleep for all the times
you wouldn't
let me live

the sunflower project

i do not remember the day i gave you lordship over me
somewhere
my love turned into obsession
while yours became domination
i do not remember
when i appointed you
but i will never forget snatching my existence from your palms
cutting the puppet strings and falling to my freedom
you no longer move me
now when i dance
it's not because you allowed it
but
because i know and do what i choose

you are offended because i closed off my soul to you
would you rather i continue
allowing you
to rape my grounds
of the sunflowers that bloom there
you ripped each reminder from inside of me
trapped my nutrients under your fingernails
you were careless with my harvest
your rough handling left my fields
mauled beyond recognition
had i let you stay
i would not have allowed Daddy to undo your damage
had i let you stay
i would have expected
the hand that fixed me
to be yours
when
 you were always incapable of preparing me for new fruit
in your absence
Daddy made me ready for planting
He dressed my pasture with grace
He moved with
tenderness
affection
and
intentionality
maybe i should have let you watch
how the extension of His love
restored my soul
maybe then you could
love me more like He does
nonetheless
the responsibility
to teach you to keep my grounds
to protect His work
does not belong to me –
but to Him

people were not meant to be collateral damage

clean up your mess

to her:
i know what it's like to love
him
i know what you believe
we've been through too much
not to make it
if you showed me your heart
it would look like mine
countless ruptures
innumerable contusions
it will be a wonder to you that
it still works
but acknowledge that it does
this is what i want for you
look at that beating heart
and look at yourself
how much more will you
allow it to take
trying to love a ghost
how much do you think it's
worth
to keep putting it in hands that
abuse it
will you let him beat it to
death
or will you let it beat for your
life
one or the other must happen
you are worthy of restoration
accept that he is not worthy of
you

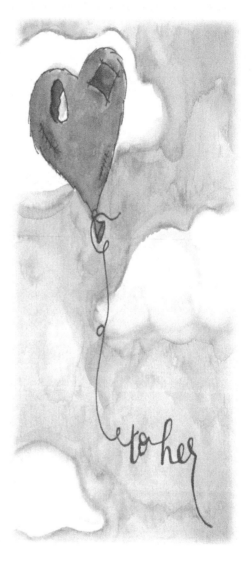

the sunflower project

i used to be ashamed that these unpleasantries
had taken root on my grounds
but because my stem did not break
i see that the unpleasantries
give me more of which to be proud
they make me more like the sunflowers around me
they give us more of ourselves to love
i am grateful now
to still be in bloom
when there were many times
my blooming was threatened
i am blessed to say
hope survived

unLYSHed

i told him my story when he asked
why i keep my body to myself
i condensed
the withering
and glorified the budding
so that he could see
i must continue to bloom
you should have seen the smile he painted
as if he was delighted to see my petals stretching before him
i closed my eyes to breathe out my relief
and opened them to find his seat empty
another
who wanted my body
without my heart

they stay together

sometimes when the time comes to speak up
my tongue still becomes tied
my past inhibitions fondle with my present aspirations
they create knots of conflict
i escape to my pen and i write
i explain
this is what still saves me

unLYSHed

i knew you were not the one
when you pinned your frustrations to my words
must you speak in riddles
why must you say so much
i was speaking to you in the tongue of my spirit
you were incapable of comprehension

you force onto me your body
as if it has no value to you
you just met me
you do not know of the storms i've weathered
of the miles i've run
or if i even function properly
yet you'll shed your clothes
and come into my temple
as if this body is home to you
as if this body
is worthy of your own
i used to feel belittled
i wondered why you could not love *me*
i'm only beginning to realize
that not only can you not love me
you have not yet learned to love yourself

u n L Y S H e d

the Inhabitant of my heart
does not mix with every spirit
and His tenancy is perpetual
His lease will never expire
you may not enter
lest the two of you
get along

      i am not my own

the sunflower project

i thought you and i would bloom together
but you have yet to even become a flower
you are no longer welcome
nor are all the things you made me feel
you are much easier to be rid of
than they

unLYSHed

you are unaware
of what it took me to get here
to love this body
to forgive my own sin
to detach the souls of strangers
from my own
you could not know
how i have blossomed
you could not know
how i have healed
you have no right
to ask me to go backwards
to give you your pleasure
i will have to live with me
when you leave

i will not be a dissatisfied tenant

the sunflower project

i'm stronger now
sunflowers are budding in my hair
and in my skin
i thought that would be respected
maybe it is
but people still leave

the world would rather we
touch
but not feel
kiss
but not taste
sometimes it seems as if
i'm standing in the midst of
a strange breeze
i reach to grasp it
but it does not reciprocate the grip
it would rather brush against me in drift
than take me away with it
sometimes
it's as if i'm a stranger
because i reject the world's way
i want to
ride along the breeze
to touch and to feel
to kiss and to taste
one without the other won't do for me
and yet
both at once have been
impossible to attain

the sunflower project

the blossoms are beautiful
but the loneliness
is an affliction
it cripples

i've grown
to celebrate the fact
that i've never owned the heart of a lover
that instead of being a heart breaker
i was always
a heart healer
i never had anyone give up something because of their love for me
but rather because of what they learned from me
they held what they did love
closer

HOLD WHAT YOU closer

i made myself smile at *her*
i felt my heart thanking me
for giving the simplest act of kindness
i so thoughtlessly offer to other people
to myself

hello LYSH

u n L Y S H e d

i am neither victim nor culprit
just blooming

the sunflower project

the sunflower project

dear LYSH,

i missed your laughter

unLYSHed

the world will never be kind
but regardless of the flowers that bud around me
i am responsible for what i allow to take root within me
i cannot make excuses
for the weeds
for the dry spots
for the dead zones
i should not spread my seed
if it is poisoned with my untended wounds
it is for me to find a way to bloom
despite

the sunflower project

they were surprised when i showed them
the wiring and taping
that held my stem upright
they say
"you've always bloomed so beautifully"
i smile and respond
"i was not without help"

somebody was praying
    somebody is still praying

unLYSHed

for some reason
i still draw the broken
and i want to love them
i want for us to
heal together
for some reason
i still find myself in briar patches of my familiar
for some reason i still
hang my head
in these times i now waste no time
i look directly to the Son

the sunflower project

the morning after, i woke
waiting to feel the familiar hands of guilt and shame find their way to
my neck to squeeze out my liveliness
make me corpselike
make me cold
i waited for my voice to sound in my head of how simply
imbecilic i had been
how dirty i had become
i waited to hear that i was unworthy of love
not from the man who would leave my bed cold
not from the God who gave me this heart
and especially not from myself
i expected the relapse to kill me
instead i found a note from my Daddy
He said
not this time

      greater grace

the budding
is the wakening
the maturing
all roads have always led back to Him
the young girl who loved the idea of love
finally found it
and activated it
when she was getting too close
the forbidding ways of this world tried to take Him too
but the gift of that love
is irrevocable
her place in His arms
could never be filled by another
we are all searching
the budding is the finding
of wholeness
acceptance and
identity
it is the understanding of never fully having understanding
but fully having faith
it is the becoming of a sunflower
i grew weary of emulating daisies
lilacs
and roses
i was meant to be a sunflower

unLYSHing

u n L Y S H e d

and so
the sunflower project and the Lily of the Valley
became reacquainted

you have no idea
what i have done
and what i have allowed
waiting for man to love me
and losing
 love for myself
you have no idea how it felt
to acknowledge the receipt of the kind of love
that i aspired to have
the kind that refuses to quit
that continually wants me
that heals me
and protects me
you persecute me for it
you reject and abuse me for it
but
you have no idea what it means to love me
and you have no idea what i will do
to defend and preserve the love that i have found

the love my Father gives

i remember being caged
i remember refusing to approach the bars
guilt
shame and
fear
each glowed with the ability to singe my hope if i dared to approach
the threat of addressing them induced my stillness which
 created indentation fit for my body in the mattress foam
and i lay
contently discontent
until one day
i lifted my head to speak to the guard
to ask for a thinner pillow
an even poorer place to exist
imagine how my insides lurched
how nauseous i began to feel
to see that the enforcer behind my caging
had my face

some nights i would wake up moaning in discomfort
the pain was like a vacuum opening in my chest
my heart
an open portal
 looking for *something*
but sucking in oblivion
my soul scratched at the walls of my body
begging for an exit
clawing for freedom
my heart
needed to be fulfilled
with purpose
dissatisfaction woke me from my sleep
i was yearning
aching
longing
for bigger

my writing motivated my escape
from *dear Daddy* to the words of my story that He helped me string
together
they broke the glass around my ability to comprehend and
i felt petals form within my crown
there was more
to perceive
to accept
and to discover
through my pen He invoked a wonder in me it
shined in my eyes which held the stars and their wishes
my fingertips tingled with excitement to attempt to describe life on the
outside
i was eager
to see the sunlight
determined to break free from the cage
i stood with the confidence of a 9-month-old child
took my first steps from my bed toward the bars
the ground shook in response to the waking of a woman
the force caused me to stumble
i shook with terror from the ground
until the hands of grace lifted me up
i approached the bars and raised a trembling hand to push
they collapsed around me
i dove to the ground before the ceiling caved
i came to my feet
but i was still in darkness
i determined to fumble through
i moved quickly
the walls whispered to me to go back
i sped up
the ground produced roots to cause me to trip

i crashed to the ground and the voices got louder
terror ripped its way into my heart
doubt began to fester
i heard fear's footsteps building behind me
and felt a chill i had not felt before
an unwanted presence i believed was coming for me
i cried out for help
i asked for the Son and saw my hands begin to glow
i stretched them forth and saw the way
mercy pulled me to my feet
and i moved
the walls did not cease their taunting
the ground did not stop its ploys
but my feet did not stop
i drove them into the ground, my heart pounding in my ears
i got winded
the way became long
and just as i needed hope
a light which mine favored peered into the tunnel
i ran toward it and found it looming over me
i dug my hands into the walls mustered up my strength and pulled my
body up
i moaned out in pain
my strength was not enough
i called out to Daddy to borrow some of His and We fought
We climbed
We pressed on into daylight
He pulled my body from the pit
i lay on the ground's surface and exhaled
then stood to marvel at the grass growing beneath my feet
the flowers budding as i picked up my head
i raised my hands in praise
it was
like i had been reborn

renewed
i stepped forward into my liberty
one hand holding onto grace and the other onto mercy
the Son's love shining all around me
gratitude dripped from my lips for this day
the day of my unLYSHing

nervous fingers rapped the table-top
my leg bounced with anticipation
i looked to and from the door waiting for the special arrival
i was dressed in my best
my tongue laced with apologies
my pen ready to produce new promises
and a mind to put my words into action
i hoped she would come home - take her place in my chest and
give me a chance to be who i knew i could be
i was ready to deliver – i was ready to be faithful
i just needed her trust

my heart was coming to dinner

unLYSHed

the need to fall in love over again renews with every season

do not shy away from the pursuit

the sunflower project

sit down
undress
become bare and look
at how you rise and fall constantly
at the way you curve endlessly
kiss the scars if you find them
caress the bruises if they are there
then consult the Creator
ask Him for internal mirrors
that reflect in your eyes that you might see *those petals*
the ones you are proud of
and the ones you are afraid to touch
take them in
each part of you
keep looking
decide which are in need of your attention
and which could use a bit of your love
continue to look at your whole self
until what looks back at you
is your kind of beautiful

u n L Y S H e d

this skin
if liquified
would drip
of brown sugar and honey
it would shimmer in glitter and gold
hands that are anxious
packaged her improperly

mishandled her

devoured her

slow down
marvel at how she mirrors light
savor the richness of her taste
she possesses a flavor that becomes richer with time
day after day
the brighter she shines
this skin
is meant to be kissed with tenderness
do not be anxious
do not be blind
know that this skin is a gift
her wearer will give back
to you
if you would allow

the fountain in your garden overflows with healing
her waters consistently rise in abundant supply
she is scented with necessity
she draws others in
a sip
is powerful
it alters the functioning of the mind
a sip
is soothing
it tickles the throat
when healing rushes over you
do not resist her effects
let her blanket you in overflow
quench your thirst
rearrange your core
til who raises her head and pats dry her lip does so
in
wholeness

u n L Y S H e d

unbridle your tongue – say what you need

i know the tears sometimes surprise you
your heart is happy now
but your mind remembers *then*
do not be ashamed
that as bright as the Son is shining
you sometimes still feel cold
just know
that feeling is temporary
the Son will shine forever
and when you are ready to welcome
His light once again
when you are ready for His warmth to permeate your space
you won't have to ask
you will find that it
that He
was always in waiting for you

unLYSHed

forgiveness is like new ground
it is the brushing away of dead petals
it is the plowing that creates
a place to plant new seed
a place to bear new fruit
do not hold on to that which is lifeless
nor that which makes your soul bitter
think of that new ground
think of that new seed
you are worthy of the plentiful season
it is calling for you

the sunflower project

everyday is not a good day
everyday is not easy
but everyday
i will try

      forward movement

u n L Y S H e d

i am no longer a chameleon
i do not disappear into the man next to me
or into the needs of others
i am a woman
and these days
with a pen in my hand
no bra
bare feet
wild hair
this smile
in this skin
i have never felt more
like myself

the sunflower project

i am the woman
          who needs to be touched

let me explain

i'm everything you believe i am
amazing
beautiful
and
searching -
my Daddy says i'm worth the blood of His Son,
my daddy says i'm worth the moon and the sun
but i break down daily til i'm scattered throughout twilight
swallowed by dusk
and regurgitated by the atmosphere as a gently used star
i usually give myself away at the discounted price –
and
i do
believe that i'm
worth more, just
been dulled for so long i've forgotten how to shine my best
i'm unable to find myself somewhere between my past and my present
i lose my footing reaching for my future with quicksand as my grounding
and i *sink*
clutching my significance along with my breath to find that oxygen has been
replaced with particles of desperation,
i struggle
this crown gets heavy
it's my birthright but i was loved wrong
and now i
can't remember how to wear it
i'm not used
to walking as if i'm worthy
some days i crumble beneath the pressure,
and it
breaks my *bones*
when i watch them heal - *i do it alone*
a piece of me dies every time that they leave me
and they all did leave me
now my fragments are resurrected, but i'm not sure how to be whole again

i want to explain –
these bruises are mine
i *crash* every time i try to prove
that i'm someone with whom he should stay
that i'm not the one who should wake to his rejection
my first robbed me of my confidence and since that time i
lost my
mind
then found it
and plucked away everything he taught me
i finally love the marks the rest put on me, but i was prisoner so long i'm still
getting used to the sunlight
sometimes i frown
and i know that i'm frazzled
but i'm excited because i'm standing
i'm
moving
though it be blindly
and i apologize for bumping into you
but now that we're here i'll say
i
wonder about you
i wonder if you see me with more than your eyes
if you notice me squinting and instead of taking advantage of my
disadvantage
if you'll help me bring my world into focus that i may see me better, see *you*
better
if you can make out my bruises
and see them
not as eyesores
but rather as stories to be told and patiently await their healing while
listening to how i fell, recognizing that you didn't find me on the ground
i wonder if you'll look past my frazzled state and ask me how i got this way,
how long i remained caged,
i wonder if you'll take note of my distortion and rather than be disgusted,
listen to how i broke my bones and retaught myself to walk
i wonder if you'll discern

that i get anxious when the sun goes down because i'm still afraid of the
darkness and then
i wonder if you'll hold me
if you'll hide me in the sanctuary of your arms and warm me with
compassion til my trembling ceases then remind me
that *i am the light in the dark*
i wonder if you won't find humor in my tears but rather give them new
reason to stain my cheeks,
this time in happiness and *not in brokenness*
i wonder if you'll look at me
and know
that i'm better at loving you than i am at loving myself
that i'd die for you even though it means sacrificing myself
that everyday i will need saving
and if instead of running to my rescue you will stand behind me reminding
me of my strength
until i've reconnected with the Son
i want to explain
that i am everything you believe i am
beautiful
amazing
searching
i am nowhere near together, but i no longer compromise on my *wholeness*
i smile so openly because once the desire was stolen from me
i'm still learning and loving parts of myself but my heart has room for you
only if you can see
i do not want your pity, i want your understanding
i'm standing here
seeing you
wondering if you can really see me
i wonder
if you are the one
who will
who was meant
to
stay

my mind had been lying to me
i believed my cage was cozy
in reality my heart and my desires were much too big for its space
i was a dreamer – and a believer
but my logical thinking would step up to deny the seed of my fervor its
chance to be planted
*but what is logic next to the God who created the people who defined
it*
He is love and promises
so i believe in love and promises
believing in Him is believing in the unthinkable
and it was absurd to believe i was deserving
insane to consider myself worthy
ridiculous to hope in love
and so because of Him *i committed all the more*
to dreaming
to believing
to writing
and to waiting
on *him*
the petals stained with untruths were plucked from my center
made more room for
the ones God planted, now budding with newness and actuality
because in reality
grace is sufficient
even for me

    He approves my "bigger"

u n L Y S H e d

i have yet to experience the kind of romantic love
i dream of having as my own
so, before i crawl under my sheets
i dab on my favorite scent and gloss my lips
preparing to meet him
in the realm of my desires
there
love is as honest as i wish it to be
it's as raw as i need it to be
it's much more beautiful
than what i've been given

do not wake me for less

i cannot yet prove your existence
my eyes have yet to meet yours
but i hold one suitcase of hope
the other hand
holds one of passion
the way that i believe you will come for me
keeps the lead in my feet
the weight in my hands
and the others
forsaken
i will not suffer for
my impatience
again
instead
i will wait for your
arrival

i hear your heartbeat
i see your eyes poorly hiding glistening wonder peering and shining
into mine,
and i feel you –
as you move closer and since you refuse to stop your stare,
you haven't touched me
yet my body is responding to your presence
taste me and see
bravely drink deeply
from my teeming chalice of intoxicating glory
let me trickle into your soul –
fill you with the love you never knew existed
i wonder
if my fermented truth will be strong enough to inebriate you –
if the effervescence from my essence mixing into yours is evidence of
your incapacity to deny what you feel for me
will one be the other's dangerously addictive concoction with which
we will toast to forever
have i been set aside for you
and if it is such that i am enough, to fill you with the liquid courage to
reveal yourself to me that means that you are not only you but you are
him
and i have longed for
him
the deliverer of God's priority packaged promise of his heart in my
hands
him
whose existence i have protected in my spirit,
hence the embers that glow beneath the lost love pile hidden behind
my hopeful eyes
him
who'll cradle my fragility in his rugged hands, rock me in the comfort
of the surety of his love

lay me down on pillows of soft promises
where i'll drift into the sweetest slumber dreaming of beholding his
face only to wake and find him next to me –
him
who'll refrain from punishing me for being trusting
but rather
touch me
knowing i'll crumble beneath his fingertips then
catch my falling parts before they touch the ground
force me back into myself
then into oneness with him and the God who gave him the authority to
keep me together
him –
who'll look at my nakedness as artwork to be beheld by him only
a sculpture carved and to be held by him only
he'll
hover over my bruises,
ponder over my scars
connect with my sensitivity, meditate on my every thought, reach to
touch my creativity and identify with my heart
he'll gaze at me in awe until my body gives birth to hidden secrets that
bear his name
then heat and revert me to clay making me putty in his hands
he'll reshape me,
mold me the same way because to him
i was never flawed,
with the exception of his name engraved on my heart and
his lips printed on my scars
him
who'll reward my exposure in the sacrifice of his pride on the altar
built on the parts of him he's always tried to hide and as our
lovesmoke stains the sky he'll reveal his abdomen to unveil the space
his rib once occupied before God fashioned it into
me –

him
whose walls i burned and whose love is a fortress around me,
who released his smile to me and entrusted me with his fears
who sheds his brawniness in my sight and rests vulnerably and
defenselessly in *my* arms that are anointed to form a shield of
protection around *him*
me with him shakes down settling
it blows up mediocrity
he, i will forever be thankful for
for obeying and conforming to the ways of God
for walking in his ordered steps over the threshold that led him to me
for sipping from my cup when the loss of control made his bones cold
with terror
for believing
that God would restore him with warmth he's never experienced if he
trusted Him more than he trusted himself
i thank him
for trusting Him more than he trusts himself
and
for being home
and laughter
and passion
and strength
and safety
and healing
and compelling
and complete –
for being the revelation of love unrealized
i thank *Him*
for he
that is you
who is now
mine

the sunflower project

he will listen
with patience
til the dissonance in my melody becomes his favorite part of my song

u n L Y S H e d

i'm in need
of the steam and the warmth only you will bring
and a shot
just won't do

he will be my espresso

the heat my body makes under your fingertips will soften my parts
it will make me a pool beneath your feet
when you smile
i will evaporate and become bubbles of ecstasy with your happiness as
the film around my own
your i love you's will reform me
so that i can give you the same touch
and the same smile
those i love you's
will stand as some of the most solid truth i've ever known

u n L Y S H e d

i don't want the moon
just stand with me under its light
be my warmth despite the coolness after dusk
share your heart with me
rob me of my darkness and replace it with your illuminated honesty while
our heartbeats drum louder than the creatures in the night
i don't want the ocean
only to drown in your affections for me, to be knocked down by waves of our
vibrations, quivering in my bones when you speak my love language
to be taken under –
to have my lungs filled with the freely flowing substance that is rivers of
your splendor
and to be
revived by our forever
i don't want the air
i'd rather lose my breath each time you close your lips on mine
hold them captive
til i'm lightheaded, suffocating as a result of your closeness –
i am prepared
for the nights the clouds cover the moon's face
the nights we struggle to see one another because circumstance darkens our
world
i understand there will be high tide –
that being knocked down by painful words running from the others' mouth
could lead to us being overcome by the waves
i expect the air to sometimes become heavy with tension and try to choke out
our happiness
even then
i won't want promises you cannot keep
nor items you cannot attain
i do want passion that creates its own light
i do want effort on which we set sail
i do want love that breathes out life
i want this
in its realest form
i want this
to last

they told me to stop believing in you
fairytales don't exist
sometimes they get to me
i've waited for so long
fumbled so much
suffered so much
and i've never seen even a glimpse of you
i look to God for answers
He rushes in with your spirit
each time He allows me to feel you
my patience is renewed
i assume
you won't see yourself as prince charming when we finally meet
my presence may snatch your attention
but my enthusiasm for loving
may lead you to turn your head in thought
considering my ways
you may watch
and think me to be peculiar
but because you *are* him
i know you won't move
because you *are* him
you will reach to protect me and a sword will form in your hand
because you *are* him
you will affirm all that i believe in the way that you love me
you will fight your way to me
obstacle by obstacle
until we finally touch
you may not believe that you are prince charming
but that matters not
when you give your heart to me
i will make you "King"

if ever you were brave enough to love
you're a hero
knowing that to crack open the casing to every sensitive and sacred
thing within
you
and to give access to an imperfect being
may mean that there could be vandalism
robbery
or a need for eviction
and you let them touch anyway
i admire you
because you wear capes of vulnerability
the emblem of trust
and you believe in the greater good
that love heals all things

the sunflower project

queen
i dug through life's debris of
almost
maybe
 and *not good enough*
to find you
discovered and dismembered
your cage with the jaws of
hope -
demanded that the
fear chains that bruised your soul
release you from their custody
and *beheld* you
the *real* you
the *freed* you
for the first time
it moves me to see
you are no longer at rest

u n L Y S H e d

the veil was removed from my eyes
the days where my sights were stuck on almost lovers and things of the past
have become something old
i tried something new
i borrowed God's eyes so i could see you like He does
and just the sight of you
blew me away
i can now
behold you
in all of your esteemed beauty
in your regality and splendor
in your humor and your light
i honestly can't believe it took me so long
to begin
to choose
you
i know
i forced you into a den of ravenous wolves and left you to be devoured
ignorantly believing that they
only had intentions for play i
pushed you from uncomfortable heights into raging waters
expecting you to float though i gave you no life jacket i hand tossed your
heart
made it shareable
assuming gluttony would be no man's choice of sin, yet i stood by
and watched
each
feast
i pulled you from top shelf then poured and placed you into immature hands
assuming a sip would make a child a man and
he turned his nose in disgust every time

where was my mercy

i do not recall asking what you felt or needed
taking the opportunity to speak on your behalf escapes me

i looked at my knees and found no imprints from them meeting the ground in
prayer with you
looking and waiting for heaven to open up and produce its answer
i never looked out for you
i owe you
attention
i owe you
my time
time spent
dedicated to scouring through
the rubble from the wrecking to
find you
you deserve to be seen
to have your wants at your fingertips
and your needs consistently unfolding on your tongue
for them to be recognized and respected
by me and then by them
you deserve to be found
i should've protected you
should've loved you
but now i know
that to love another is not to lose oneself
and i'm sorry for
leaving you behind
but
today we celebrate
because my ears have been made sensitive to the wailing from your soul
i have pinned your desires to my chest
and plastered images of your smile throughout my mind
today i vow
never to forget you again
i vow
never to overlook you again
i vow
to exchange surviving for living
never to pressure you into settling
to speak up when things aren't working

no matter the level of commitment or amount of time spent
to protect your heart with your body and to never feel obligated to share
either against God's will
i vow to give you bubble baths
and glasses of wine
to burn your favorite candles
let you unwind
and provide your escape from the rest of the world with designated time to
put your pen to paper
i vow to make a home in our closet where we can call down heaven for a
meeting with our Creator
i promise to help you stay planted in every season until
we have heard from our Creator
i promise to become one with you and every petal of the sunflower in bloom
within you
i do
take you
to have and to hold *closely*
to love and to cherish *fiercely*
for richer or poorer despite
in sickness and in health without regard
til death call us to glory with God
from this day forward
i will
ever
give
you
love

worthy *of it all.*

they will ask me who i am
i will consider the power in the question that is mine for the taking as i
prepare to answer
it will excite me
the words will form in a puddle on my tongue
and pour out of me in orgasmic flow as i confess
i am the shattered and the healed
i am the timid and the liberated
i carry childlike wonder but am in every way a woman
i am the trapped and the triumphant
i am the fearful and the fearless
i am everything you want and likely *more than you can handle*
i am impregnated with the fullness of life and i have finally come to term
see promise crowning between my legs
fruition peeks its head preparing its entrance into this world
my hands grip onto love
my brow drips with anticipation of the responsibility that will soon be mine
i cry out
for the moments i feel pain but i *continue to push*
i need to hear the cry
of the gift God placed
inside of me
i will labor
i will cradle His delivered covenant in my bosom
i will be mother to life
and life will shine all around me
they will ask me who i am
and i will tremble at the power given me
to answer such a question
i will say
i used to be prisoner
today i am freed
i am unLYSHed

here are my sunflower's seeds
they are scattered throughout these pages
i prayed for you to hold their truth
i prayed for God's hands in the wind to deliver them into the gardens
of those who
had not yet bloomed
prayed for them to travel to cold, dead grounds
and to pollute them with the evidence of His
love
the love
that
inspired the planting
withstood the withering
and sustained the blossoming
His love unLYSHed
the sunflower project
because of love
i am whole

about the author

unLYSHed is a poet, visionary, and love enthusiast. At the age of 22, unLYSHed experienced a trauma that upset her perspective on life; that, in addition to years of mishandling and being abused in romantic love and relationships, led her to hide the trauma she could not overtly express in poetry. After feeling spiritual liberation by an expression of her truth, unLYSHed presented to her campus of Clark Atlanta University a theatrical event where she shared her work publicly for the first time. This made plain for unLYSHed where her passion lay, and she made a commitment to continue to write. What was once a means of escape, became a vital part of her identity that initiated deeper connection with God, healing, and a journey to self-love, self-discovery, freedom, and the claim to worthiness. Years later, unLYSHed wrote and published *the sunflower project*, and secured the title of author. unLYSHed has a mission to continue to walk in purpose by granting her heart its opportunity to speak, pouring out her truth to inspire others to embark on their own journeys to healthiness, happiness and wholeness – as they each deserve.

u n L Y S H e d

about the book

the sunflower project is a collection of poems that tell the story of phases of life; growing from the seed of innocence and naivety, to almost withering into nothingness with the loss of self-love and self-worth; then being revitalized by rediscovery and restoration and unfolding petals that are kissed by the sunshine of freedom, healing and the reclaiming. the sunflower project tells the story of love and loss, faithfulness and faithlessness, brokenness and abandonment, and finally introduces the rebirth and the determination to becoming centered, whole, and victorious in existence once again. the sunflower project was written in the hopes that readers would see themselves in its pages, acknowledge their heart's needs, and join the writer in embracing all of the petals that symbolize different facets of their identity worthy of love and attention; building a stem of resilience despite life's storms; and committing to continually tracking the Son under whom there is greater grace.